Hindsight

Hannah Morgan

Presentation by *BookLeaf Publishing*

Web: www.bookleafpub.com

E-mail: info@bookleafpub.com

ISBN: 9789357614207

First edition 2022

*Dedicated to my grandparents Anne,
Lorraine and Jeff x*

ACKNOWLEDGEMENT

Thank you to my wonderful family for their endless support. I'd also like to thank my amazing friends, who continue to offer daily inspiration and a shoulder to lean on.

PREFACE

Throughout this short collection, my poems cover an array of topics - mostly because I am rather indecisive and couldn't settle on one particular theme! My inspiration for writing has always originated from experiences that have provoked a deep emotion, both the highs and lows of life.

Grief was perhaps the most overwhelming emotion I was experiencing whilst writing; it was due to this that I decided now was the right time to produce this compilation. Yet only two poems directly focus on this – 'The bouquet I gift to you' and 'Still'. Instead, I looked for distractions using both my memories and my surroundings as a creative stimulus. Hindsight is a gift and writing these poems has served as a powerful reflective tool, helping me to process some of the challenging situations most of us will come to face.

A ribbon running throughout my poetry is nature. Having lived in the city all of my life, nature has always felt like a source of escapism, a more pure and simple way of living. I hope that whilst you are reading, you can find some relation to the words and encourage you to reflect on your own experiences.

Love /// Loss

I knew your thoughts before your marvellous tongue
had time to translate them.
I became more invested with every detail
of your life, every complement, oh and every
time I heard your infectious laugh.

Every insecurity was a privilege and a promise
from me to you that I could dissolve it.
You consumed my thoughts, eating away
my previous attachments and desires, until
all became a mirror image of you.

You too stayed. But you were unaware that I was waiting.
I gave you the attention you craved and you assumed
that this was a fair trade for your presence in my life.
You, a delectable poison that I consumed happily,
in full knowledge of the decay you would cause.

Now my mind tries to heal, to mend the tears
of my self-esteem. I stitch with gold,
stronger and more beautiful than you will ever be.

Am I your temptation or remedy?

My arms extend in welcome embrace, but I hold too tightly.
You crush under the weight of my attention.
As you push in closer, I'm only pulling you under.
I am the disinfectant which both stings
and mends.
Am I your temptation or remedy?

My eyes they dazzle when licked by salty tides.
You tell me you want to dive deep into those
black holes.
Whilst searching for pearls,
you'd be swept away by the ferocious tides of
my ruminations.

How long will it last,
when each moment of pleasure
is clouded by a hazy smoke.
I bring you clarity.
I am the sun that dissipates the mist,
too close and you'll scald.

My words carry magic,
enchanting your empty mind.
My silence always makes the most noise,
penetrates through your core.
Leaves you wanting more.
Is it me you adore?

Falling out of love (F.O.O.L)

3

Yes falling out of love with you
was never easy for me to do.
So I'd like to share my adaptation
of yet another one of your cancellations,
because back then I still did see
how poorly you were treating me,
but content in the knowledge you'd come around
after having your fun in the adults playground.
A heartfelt message would get me by
with that one occasion I saw him cry.
My glass heart was yours for just a minute
until you dropped it and I watched it plummet.

The shards of his words cut deep, cruel.
Yet it meant today I am no longer his fool.

Ice

They shine like diamonds as they plop
into the liquor.

I swirl the glass around, the
miniature glaciers clicking against
the crystal. They chip at the fragile glass.

Not quite completely immersed, as they
radiate their cool.
They too will melt away, just as you did.

Timekeeper

5

You rest between the big and small hands
of the clock,
preventing the minutes from passing.
The alarm never sounds

Solar

The star who shoots across my mind
carrying all my wishes and desires

No longer do I need to stare up to the sky.
You help me connect the dots
forming intricate constellations

Be my majestic meteorite,
burning through the galaxy.
Come crash into me

Gravity disappears when it's just you and I,
I'm weightless.
All my troubles space junk drifting away deep
through the universe

Venus grins

Every part of me orbits around you,
so when will the planets align?

Loving Someone

The year was 1975 when I first realised
I couldn't be more in love with You.
Other People may Talk! about Paris,
but we didn't need to leave The City
to find our Happiness.
When I am By your side,
I don't need any Medicine
to calm my Frail state of mind.
Because you make me feel like I've lostmyhead
when you tell Me "you're Mine."
To be Inside your mind,
to hear The Sound of your heart,
no this is something that M.O.N.E.Y could never buy

You

There are some people who on first meeting you instantly
recognise as
home.
There is nothing to take nor give,
an equilibrium that is reached.

There are some with whom you find yourself;
words that nourish,
glowing interests you had long forgotten about,
the eyes for which you can see your own reflection.

Those people whose
smile
triggers a reflex rush of oxytocin,
flooding your body with calming currents of understanding.

That person who makes
the shortest day of the year the most dreaded.

(as I know I have less seconds to dream about
you)

Performance

Let's pretend that you want me
as much as your body craves mine.
Act as though your kisses
have come from a place of longing rather than lust.
Let your fingers dance over my spine, cup every curve,
you make me gasp with every misplaced caress.
Can you sense my accuracy
as I carefully deliver my rehearsed steps of affection?
Your sweat mixes with mine to create a greasy film,
a barrier to molecular contact.

I wouldn't want to get too close

Medicinal

My creator,
performing your sorcery
You delighted in alchemy,
sculpting me with cold hands
until I was the most enchanting
Elixir

Shower anxiety

The warm water falls,
droplets racing each other as they tumble.
I turn the tap hotter,
hotter to simply try and feel again.
And I stand.
And I think.
And I feel.

I realise I have lived with a perpetual wave of nausea,
convening in my stomach.
Reaching for the soap, I notice the gentle vibrating tremor
that my mind has been neglecting.
I scrub at my scalp, expecting to wash away the thoughts
residing at the roots.

For those minutes, I seem to analyse every word in every sentence,
every grammar flaw I have typed,
every time I didn't smile or perhaps
I smiled too much?
Sometimes I let my mind wander to the darker times, for the lighter
ones
are much too gentle and I am numb to those now.

My cool rapid breaths
smoky steam pockets.
It surrounds me like a veil, both protective and suffocating.
I turn the shower off and let the icy air hit me.

The steam dissipates and my feelings follow shortly after.

The bouquet I gift to you

Fragrant sage and rosemary,
the scents of remembrance that
will linger on the pads of my fingers
which once intertwined with yours.
A stem of hyssop, an offering in memory
of all the sacrifices you made for us.
I steal a pink carnation,
press it between the pages of your recipe book,
so that I will taste you in each meal I cook.
White poppies, whose petals will fall to form
a pillow for your everlasting slumber.
The seeds will scatter by your grave.
Next summer they bloom,
bursting with memories.

Still

I keep expecting to feel the gentle vibration
of your call,
but everything has been still since you've gone.
Your voicemails are saved to my notes,
as if I could ever forget your voice.
You echo through my thoughts.

I stare at the clock
The one we stood on your hospital table.
It glares at me as it sits in a plastic bag,
hands paralysed since
you went.

Your silence had penetrated through my tears.
An emotion so visceral, it hurt too much to stay.
Then it was me who went silent.

The new season dawns, the first maroon leaves
just about clinging to their home.
I don't think I would be able to find my voice even now.
It is you who sits in my throat, but it is me who put you there.

Amber

The golden, glistening honey
seeping from the injured bark
in an attempt to sooth its wounds

A time machine, we stare at those
relics held in honey hues

The hypocrisy of those ancient warriors,
thinking an inert gem would guard them
from the volatile actions of the fight

Now polished jewels sit warming
on the chest of a queen
sunbeams breaching the night with scattered
light

On the tube back to modern life,
the air is heavy with the heady,
musky scent of an opulent future

Is that too much?

Today, I will:
1. Not hit snooze on my alarm I deliberately set earlier than needed
2. Actually look outside at the weather before leaving the flat
3. Smile to pretend I am a morning person
4. Not moan about yet another train cancellation
5. Resist the temptation of buying a caramel latte whilst waiting for the next train
6. Make a list of all my unnecessary spending, including weekly coffee bills, whilst drinking my latte
7. Reply to those urgent emails
8. Reply to those Whatsapp messages
9. Eat something green at lunch
10. Remember to take my multivitamin
11. Increase both physical and mental flexibility through yoga
12. Find the partner of my dreams
13. Get my life together
14. Be cosy in bed by 10pm
15. Dream of all the things I plan to accomplish

Commute

A humming buzz radiating from the tracks
I sit in solitude.
Normally I rebel against this silence
with a track playing on endless repeat

The sun takes its morning stretch slowly,
swaddling the scene in a
forgiving amber gleam,
pushing against the crisp chill of autumn

Breathing deeply,
soaking up the morning petrichor.
The air nourishes, opening the forgotten pockets,
distending the tightened muscles

My mind wonders with the passing trains,
pulling away in opposite directions,
Each carriage full of the ephemerality of hope

Shapeshifter

17

The silver moon beams tonight,
transforms those hiding in the shadows.
Do you hear me howl?

Amour-propre

The moment you start to internalise that compliment,
reject the unevidenced critique.
When you feel pride in your achievements,
whilst facilitating others to reach their own.
If you can be entranced by your own reflection,
instead of the unachievable ideals.
To have forgiving self-appreciation,
whilst embracing your evolution
when hit by life's rejections.
Emotional intellect is your form of magic.

The Gallery

Feet tap steadily against the mosaic floor.
Tiny fragments held together
by tinier fragments of sand and shell.
The seemingly insignificant, holding the pieces
in beautiful display

Slumber

Days and nights merge into one.
Dreams are no longer the escapism
I once craved, for now they are the
normality that will never return.
Nightmares too are less powerful, dulled
by the reality of each waking moment.
I am merciful for each minute I gain of peace
in my summer slumber.

Insolence (based on the fragrance, Guerlain EDP)

Iris leans in, planting a sugared kiss on delicate violet.
And with that sweet peck she blooms, her petals bursting
further then she knew she could reach.
The opulent rose looks on with envy.
Her thorns prick the
juicy berries that hang low,
nuzzled against the foot of a youthful orange tree,
whose blossom is lifted by swirls of vanilla winds.

www.ingramcontent.com/pod-product-compliance
Lightning Source LLC
La Vergne TN
LVHW051250200726
843510LV00011B/1776